yarn girls'
KNITTING JOURNAL

JULIE CARLES AND JORDANA JACOBS

PHOTOGRAPHS BY ELLEN SILVERMAN
ILLUSTRATIONS BY DANIELLA COHN AND GAIL CADEN

POTTER STYLE

D0842286

Text
copyright © 2004 by Julie Carles
and Jordana Jacobs. Photographs copyright © 2004 by Ellen Silverman. Illustrations by
Daniella Cohn and Gail Caden. Design by Jan
Derevjanik. From the book *The Yarn Girls' Guide
to Kid Knits* by Julie Carles and Jordana Jacobs
published by Clarkson Potter/ Publishers
www.clarksonpotter.com
isbn 1-4000-5396-X

Contents

the yarn girls' guide to the fundamentals

Has it been a long time since you picked up a pair of knitting needles? If so, you may be a bit rusty on the rudiments. Face it, we all get confused and forget things we have learned—even if we just learned them yesterday. Our goals are to make knitting as easy as possible and to enable you to create a sweater—start to finish—without a million trips to your local knitting store or tears and frustration. This chapter provides instructions on the basic techniques we use throughout the book. If you are a new knitter, or if you're a bit out of practice, this is where you'll turn for directions on how to knit, purl, cast on, and bind off. If you have forgotten how to make a slip knot or do a shrimp stitch, if you're not sure how to increase or decrease, or can't quite recall any of the other fundamental tools for making a knitted garment, you're in the right place. And whether this is a refresher course or your first foray into the pleasures of knitting, we promise to keep it simple.

By the way, for you lefties out there, don't be intimidated. These directions are universal, and we teach righties and lefties to knit exactly the same way. If, however, you feel you want to alter the motions slightly to compensate, go ahead—do what feels comfortable for you.

You may also have seen or heard about the European method of knitting, in which you knit with yarn wrapped around your left index finger to make a new stitch rather than wrapping the yarn around the needle with the right hand. All the illustrations and instructions in this book are based on the American method, which is how we knit and what we teach our students. If you already know how to knit in the European method, continue to do so if that's what you're comfortable with—these patterns will work equally well for you. Just make extra sure your gauge is correct.

SLIP AND CAST ON

Even before you begin to knit, you must cast the necessary number of stitches onto your needle. To do this, you have to measure out a length of yarn for a "tail," which will become your cast-on stitches. The length of the tail determines how many stitches you can cast on; the more stitches you are casting on, the longer the tail must be. Our rule of thumb is that an arm's length–that is, the distance from your wrist to your shoulder–of yarn will yield 20 stitches on the needle. So, if you need to cast on 100 stitches, you'll need to use 5 arm lengths of yarn. It is always better to have too long a tail than too short. If your tail runs out before you have cast on the required number of stitches, you will have to start over with a longer tail. You can always cut off the remaining yarn if the tail is too long, but always leave at least 2 or 3 inches.

After you measure out the tail, make a slip knot, which will also be your first cast-on stitch. Place this on a needle, hold that needle in your right hand, and continue to cast on stitches until you have the required number on the needle.

to make a slip knot

1. Measure out the required length of yarn and, with the free end hanging, make a loop at the measured point. You should see an X. (Illus. A)

2. Grab hold of the strand of yarn that is on the top of the X and bring this strand behind and through the loop. (Illus. B)

3. Hold this new loop in one hand and pull on the loose ends to create your slip knot! (Illus. C & D)

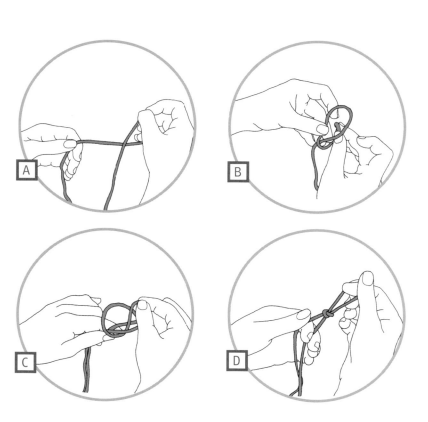

to cast on

1. Place your slip knot on a needle. Hold the needle in your right hand pointing toward the left. Hold the slip knot in place with your right index finger so it does not fly off the needle. (Illus. A)

2. Place the thumb and index finger of your left hand between the 2 strands of yarn dangling from the needle. (Your thumb should be closer to you and the index finger away from you.) Hold the dangling yarn taut with your ring and pinky fingers. (Illus. B)

3. Flip your left thumb up while guiding the needle down and to the left. A loop should form around your thumb. (Illus. C)

4. Guide the needle up through the loop on your thumb. Guide the needle over the yarn that is around your index finger and catch it with the needle. (Illus. D)

5. Guide the yarn hooked by the needle down through the loop around your thumb. (Illus. E + F) Slip your thumb out of its loop and place this thumb inside the strand of yarn that is closer to you. Pull down gently. Now you have a cast-on stitch!

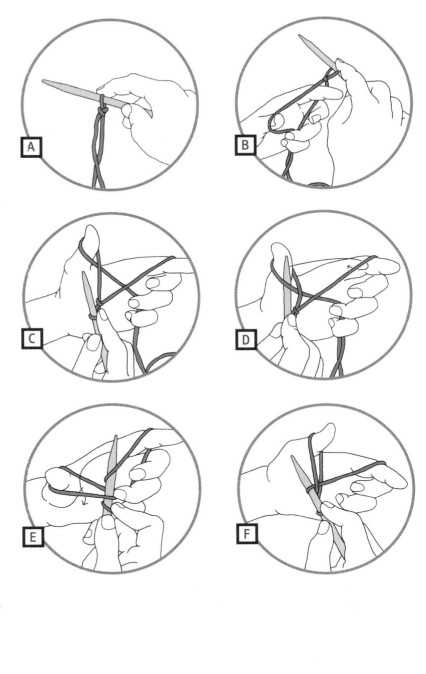

KNIT AND PURL

Knit and purl are the two stitches that make up the craft of knitting—everything else is merely a variation on one or both of these stitches. Once you master the knit and purl stitches, the world of knitting is yours to conquer.

to knit

1. Cast on the number of stitches required by your chosen pattern or 20 stitches if you are just practicing. Hold the needle with the cast-on stitches in your left hand and the empty needle in your right hand. Point the needles toward each other. (Illus. A)

2. While holding the yarn in the back, insert the right needle from front to back through the first stitch on the left needle. You will see that the needles form an *X* with the right needle beneath the left needle. (Illus. B)

3. Keep the needles crossed by holding both needles with the thumb, index, and middle fingers of your left hand. Do this by holding the right needle with the thumbnail on top facing you and the nails of the index and middle fingers underneath that right needle and facing away from you. With your right hand, pick up the yarn and wrap it under and around the bottom needle; do not wrap it around the left needle. (Illus. C)

4. Hold the yarn in place around the right needle between your right thumb and index finger and guide the right needle toward you through the center of the stitch on the left needle. (Illus. D) The right needle should now be on top of the left needle. (Illus. E)

5. Pull the remaining yarn off the left needle by pulling the right needle up and to the right so the newly formed stitch slides off the left needle to the right. You will have a newly created stitch on the right needle. (Illus. F)

6. Repeat steps 1 through 5 across the entire row of stitches.

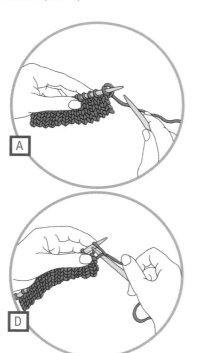

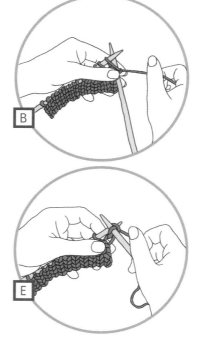

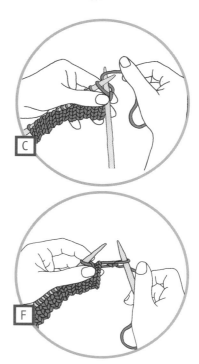

to purl

1. Hold the needle with the stitches in your left hand and the empty needle in your right hand and the loose yarn hanging in front of your work. The needles should be pointed toward each other. (Illus. A)

2. Insert the right needle back to front through the front of the first stitch on the left needle. The needles will form an *X* with the right needle on top of the left needle. Make sure the yarn is in front of the needle. (Illus. B)

3. Keep the needles crossed in the *X* position by holding both needles with the thumb, index, and middle fingers of your left hand. Do this by holding the right needle with the thumbnail on top facing you and the nails of the index and middle fingers underneath that right needle and facing away. Wrap the yarn over and around the front needle from the back, bringing the yarn around and in front of the right needle. (Illus. C)

4. Holding the yarn in place around the needle with the thumb and index finger of your right hand, push the right needle down and toward the back through the center of the stitch on the left needle. The right needle will now be behind the left needle. (Illus. D & E)

5. Pull the remaining yarn off the left needle by pulling the right needle to the right so the newly formed stitch slides off the left needle onto the right needle. (Illus. F)

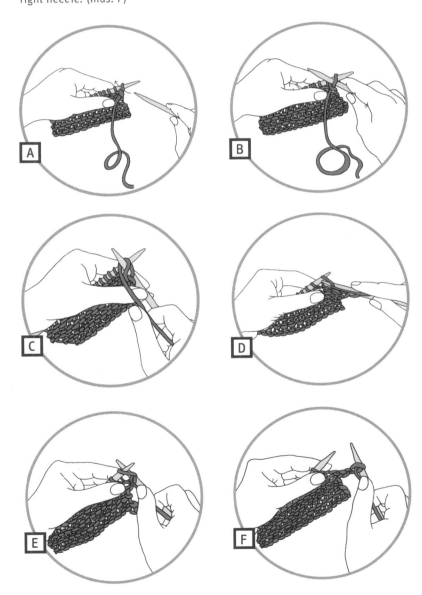

INCREASE AND DECREASE

The addition and subtraction of stitches is otherwise known as increasing and decreasing. While it is possible to increase and decrease on either the knit or the purl side of your work, there is rarely a need to do so while purling. The illustrations here show how to increase and decrease on the knit side.

INCREASING

Increasing is how you will add stitches to the number of stitches on a needle in order to add width to your knitted piece. The most common reason for increasing is shaping sleeves. A sleeve generally starts out narrow and gets wider as it gets longer. This is accomplished by adding 1 stitch to each end of the needle every several rows.

You will encounter two methods for increasing in this book. The first is the bar method, known as Make 1, or **M1,** which is our preferred way to increase while knitting sleeves. Generally, we recommend you start a bar increase 2 stitches in from the edge of your work. This means you should knit 2 stitches, then do a bar increase, then knit until there are 2 stitches remaining on the left needle, then increase again. Increasing 2 stitches in from your edge makes sewing up the seam on your sleeve much easier because you can sew down a straight line that is uninterrupted by increases.

The second kind of increase is known as knitting into the front and back of a stitch. It is a quick and easy way to increase and is generally a good choice when you want your increases at the very edge of the knitted piece. We don't like this increase for sleeves because it tends to leave a slightly jagged edge that makes sewing more difficult.

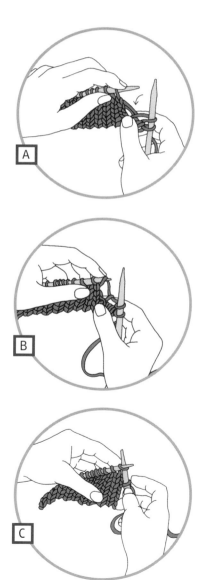

bar method
(also referred to as make 1, or m1)

1. At the point you wish to add a stitch, pull the needles slightly apart to reveal the bar located between 2 stitches. (see arrow, Illus. A)
2. With your left needle, pick up the bar from behind. (Illus. B)
3. Knit the loop you have made. Be sure to knit this loop as you would normally knit a stitch, going from the front of the stitch to the back. (Illus. C) Sometimes this stitch is a little tight and will be difficult to knit. In that case, gently push the loop up with your left forefinger, loosening the stitch and making it easier to insert your right needle.

knitting into the front and back of a stitch

1. Begin to knit into the stitch you are going to increase into. Stop when you have brought the right needle through the stitch on the left needle and it is forming the X in the front. (Illus. A) DO NOT take the stitch off the left needle as you normally would when completing a knit stitch.

2. Instead, leave the stitch on the left needle and move the tip of the right needle so it is behind the left needle. (Illus. B)

3. Insert the right needle into the back of the stitch on the left needle (Illus. C) and knit it again—wrap yarn around the back needle counterclockwise. Hold the yarn against the needle with your right hand and guide the needle toward you through the center of the stitch. The right needle should end up on top of the left needle.

4. Pull the stitch off the left needle. You now have 2 stitches on the right needle. (Illus. D)

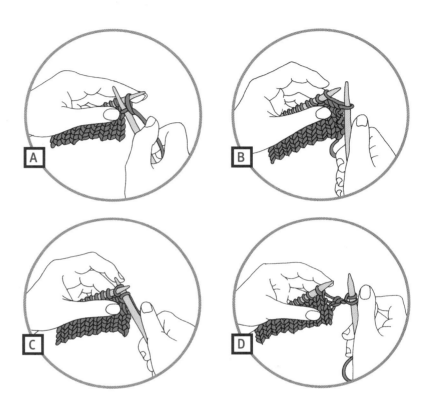

DECREASING

Decreasing is how you will reduce the number of stitches on a needle in order to narrow the width of your knitted piece. The most common use for decreases is shaping armholes and necks.

In this book, we use two methods of decreasing. The first is a slip, slip, knit, abbreviated as **SSK.** This is a left-slanting decrease. The other method is a Knit 2 together, abbreviated as **K2tog.** This is a right-slanting decrease.

slip, slip, knit

We use this method when we want our decreases to slant toward the *left.*

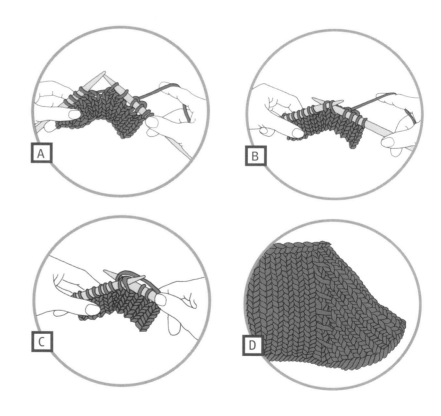

1. One at a time, slip 2 stitches as though you were going to knit them (Knitwise), to the right needle. (Slipping a stitch means that you insert your right needle into the loop on the left needle as though you were going to knit it BUT you don't complete the knit stitch; you just slide the stitch off the left needle onto the right needle.) (Illus. A)

2. Insert the left needle into the front of the 2 slipped stitches, forming an *X*, with the left needle in front of the right needle. (Illus. B)

3. Wrap the yarn counterclockwise around the back needle and knit the 2 slipped stitches together, slipping the completed new stitch onto the right needle. (Illus. C & D)

knit 2 together
(k2tog)

We use this technique when we want our decreases to slant to the *right*.

1. Working on a knit row, insert your right needle from front to back into the second and then the first stitch you want to knit together. (Illus. A)
2. Bring the yarn around the needle and complete the stitch as though you were knitting a regular stitch. (Illus. B & C)

BIND OFF

Binding off is how you get your knitted piece off the needles and prevent it from unraveling. You bind off when you are finished with your blanket, when you are shaping a neck or armholes, or when you have completed the front or back of a sweater. You can bind off on a knit or a purl row. The concept is the same either way. We illustrate how to bind off on a knit row.

1. Knit 2 stitches. (Illus. A)
2. Insert the left needle into the front of the first stitch on the right needle. Using the left needle, pull the first stitch up and over the second stitch. (Illus. B) You can place your forefinger on the second stitch to hold it in place and keep it from coming off the needle.
3. Now push that stitch off the left needle completely. (Illus. C & D)
4. Knit one more stitch and repeat the last two steps. Continue this process until you have bound off the desired number of stitches.

When you are binding off all your stitches at the end of a blanket or when you are done knitting a section of your sweater, you should have 1 loop left on the right needle. At this point, cut the yarn, leaving 3 or 4 inches, and pull the end through the remaining loop to tie it off.

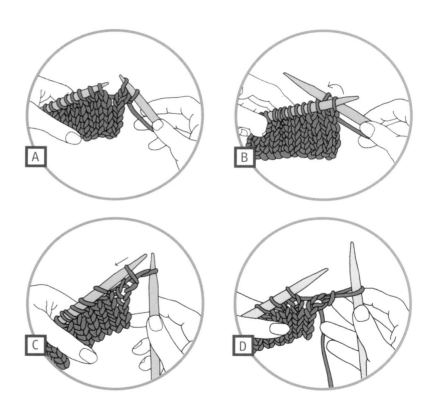

A

B

C

D

YARN OVERS

A yarn over (abbreviated YO) basically allows you to make a hole in your knitting on purpose—as opposed to those inadvertent holes made by dropping stitches. Yarn overs are generally used for lace knitting or to make a buttonhole.

yarn over before a knit

If the stitch after the yarn over will be a knit, use this method of making a yarn over:

1. Hold both needles with the fingers of your left hand and hold the yarn with your right hand in back of the right need e. (Illus. A)
2. Pull the yarn up and around the right-hand needle from the front to the back. (Illus. B) You created the yarn over, which is just a loop.

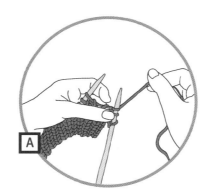

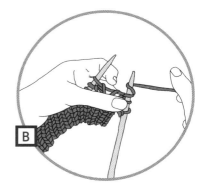

yarn over before a purl

If the stitch after the yarn over will be a purl, use th is method:

1. Hold both needles with the fingers of your left hand and hold the yarn with your right hand in front of the right need e. (Illus. A)
2. Pull the yarn up and around the needle counterclockwise, from the front to the back and to the front again. (Illus. B)

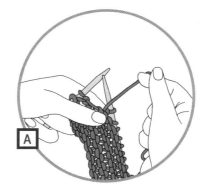

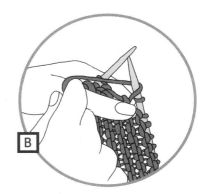

CAST ON IN THE MIDDLE OF ROW

You will need to cast on in the middle of a row when your project requires a hole in the middle of a row. We designed a hole in our bunting so a car seat or stroller straps can pass through it. Before you cast on in the middle of a row, you need to bind off those stitches on the row before. This is done exactly as you would when shaping the neck for a crew-neck pullover. This technique is also an alternative way to make buttonholes.

1. Work to where the cast-off stitches are. (Illus. A)

2. Turn work so the yarn is attached to the stitches on the left needle. (Illus. B)

3. Insert the right needle into the first stitch on the left needle and knit it, but do not take it off the left needle. (Illus. C)

4. Bring the left needle to the front and right of the stitch on the right needle and then insert the left needle into the stitch on the right needle. (Illus. D)

5. Transfer the stitch from the right to the left needle. (Illus. E)

6. You have now cast on 1 stitch in the middle of the row.

7. Repeat these steps until you have cast on the desired number of stitch-es in the middle of the row.

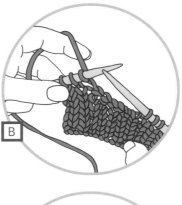

FINISHING TECHNIQUES

You can spend hours knitting row after row of perfect ribbing and flawless stockinette stitch, but all those efforts can be undermined by sloppy finishing technique. Knowing how to sew a sweater together properly is the key to whether the sweater looks handmade—or homemade. Finishing a sweater is the bane of many a knitter's existence, but it doesn't have to be. If you use the proper techniques, the process should be relatively painless and your sweater should look virtually seamless. And a final steaming, known as blocking, will smooth over any inconsistencies or bumpy seams.

Some tips:

- This may go against every instinct you possess, but sweaters are always sewn on the right side. This means that unlike regular sewing, where the two right sides of your garment are facing each other when you sew, in knitting **the right sides face out.**

- Although other people might tell you differently, we prefer **not** to use the yarn we knit our sweater with to sew it together. If your garment is sewn together properly, you will not see any of the yarn used for sewing on the right side. This means, theoretically, that you should be able to sew your black sweater together with hot pink yarn. Generally, we suggest using a needlepoint yarn in a similar color because using a different yarn allows you to see what you are doing much more clearly. And, dare we say it, it also enables you to rip out what you have done, if necessary, without inadvertently damaging the sweater itself.

Whether you are making a V-neck, turtleneck, crew neck, or cardigan, sweaters are always assembled in the same order:

1. Sew shoulder seams together.
2. Sew sleeves onto sweater.
3. Sew sleeve seams from armhole to cuff.
4. Sew side seams from armhole to waist.

Once the pieces are joined together, you can add crochet edgings, pick up stitches for a neck, create button bands for a cardigan, or embellish with other finishing touches.

sewing shoulder seams

1. Lay the front and back of your sweater flat with the right sides facing you and the shoulders pointing toward each other. If you are sewing the shoulder seams of a cardigan together, make sure the neck and armholes are facing in the correct direction, with the armholes facing away from the center and the neck toward the center. (Illus. A)

2. Cut a piece of sewing yarn approximately twice the width of your shoulder seam and thread it through a darning needle.

3. Secure the sewing yarn to the garment by making a knot with one end of the sewing yarn on the inside shoulder edge of the back of your sweater.

4. Insert the needle into the first stitch at the shoulder edge of the front of the sweater. Your needle should have passed under 2 bars and should be on the right side or outside of the work. (Illus. B)

5. Now place the needle under the corresponding stitch of the back of your sweater. (Illus. C) Next, insert the needle into the hole the yarn is coming from on the front and go under the next stitch. Then do the same thing on the back. This is how you continue to weave the sweater together. It is easier if you keep the yarn relatively loose because it is easier to see the hole your yarn is coming from. Pull the sewing yarn tight after you have 6 or 7 stitches and just loosen the last stitch before you proceed.

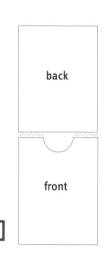

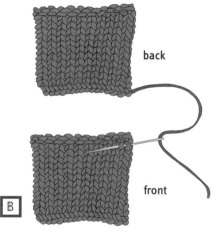

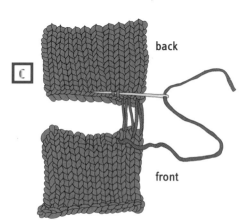

sewing the sleeves to the body

This aspect of finishing is relatively painless when sweaters are drop sleeve. This means there are no armholes. So you need to determine how many inches you need on either side to evenly sew the sleeve from the shoulder seam down the side. Before you start sewing, just place a marker at these points and adjust your sewing as you go along. You do not want the sleeve to be too narrow or too wide. You have knit the sleeve to a certain width at the top and it should, if sewn in properly, hit the right spot, but you do need to make sure.

These measurements are a guide to help you find the right spot.

0–3 months: 5″ • 3–6 months: 5.5″ • 1 year: 6″ • 2 years: 6.5″ • 3 years: 7″

IMPORTANT: WHEN YOU SEW SLEEVES ONTO THE BODY, MAKE SURE THEY COME DOWN TO THE CORRECT PLACE.

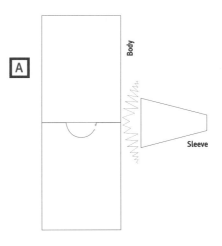

1. Cut a piece of yarn approximately 20″ long and thread it through a darning needle.

2. Attach the yarn to the body of the sweater by poking the needle through the edge of the shoulder seam you made when sewing the shoulders together. Pull the yarn halfway through and make a knot. You should now have half the yarn going down one side of the armhole and half going down the other side.

3. Find the center of the upper sleeve edge by folding the sleeve in half. With the yarn needle, pull the yarn under the center 2 bars on the sleeve. (Illus. A) Your sleeve is now attached to the body of the sweater.

4. Now you need to find 2 bars on the body of the sweater. Start at the top near the shoulder seam. This is slightly different from finding the bars on the sleeves because the bars on the sleeves are stitches and on the body, the bars will be rows. Place the needle 1 full stitch in on the body of the sweater and find the 2 bars. (Illus. B)

5. Continue sewing as for the shoulders, taking 2 bars from the body and 2 bars from the sleeve and pulling the yarn every few stitches until the sewing yarn is no longer visible and until the sleeve is sewn into the armhole. (Illus. C & D)

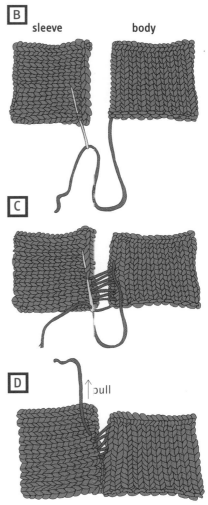

21

sewing up rolled edges

When sewing up a project that has rolled edges, you will want to finish it off so you don't see the seam when the fabric rolls. The way you do this is to sew your seam as you always do, on the right side of the work, BUT at about 1 inch or so before you reach the bottom, you must start sewing on the wrong side of the work instead of the right side. The seam will then show up on the right side, but the roll edge will cover it.

sewing side & sleeve seams

1. Cut a piece of yarn approximately twice the length of the sleeve and side seam.

2. Attach the yarn by inserting the sewing needle through the two seams at the underarm. Pull the yarn halfway through and make a knot. Half of the yarn should be used to sew the side seam and half should be used to sew the sleeve seam.

3. It doesn't matter whether you start with the body or the sleeve. For both, find the 2 vertical bars 1 full stitch in from the edge and begin the sewing process (Illus. A), taking 2 bars from one side of the sweater and then 2 bars from the other side. (Illus. B) Make sure you are going into the hole where the yarn last came out and pulling the yarn every few stitches. (Illus. C)

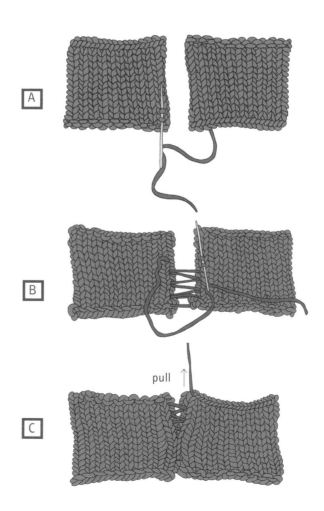

A

B

pull ↑

C

picking up stitches

Once the pieces of your sweater are joined, you need to make a nice finished edge for the neckline. If you are making a cardigan, you will also need to add button bands on each side, one with buttonholes and the other a solid strip to which you will attach the buttons. Rather than knit these elements as separate pieces that are then sewn on, we like to knit them directly onto the finished sweater. In order to do this, you must pick up stitches along the finished edges. When you pick up the stitches for a neck, you are generally picking up stitches horizontally in an already-made stitch. When picking up for button bands, you pick up the stitches vertically, in rows. Either way, the method for picking up the stitches is the same; the difference is where you place the needle to pick up the next stitch. You can pick up stitches in existing stitches (vertically Illus. A–E) or in rows (horizontally Illus. F–J).

When you are picking up stitches in stitches, as for a crew-neck pullover, most of the time you want to pick up every stitch. It is important to note that there is an extra hole between each stitch. So picking up every stitch is the same thing as picking up every other hole. If you poke your needle through every consecutive hole, you will pick up too many stitches.

When you are picking up stitches in rows, as when you are picking up button bands, you do not want to pick up a stitch in *every* row. To determine how often to pick up, note your gauge. If your gauge is 3 stitches to the inch, then you will want to pick up stitches in 3 consecutive rows, then skip 1 row and repeat this process. If your gauge is 4 stitches to the inch, you will want to pick up stitches in 4 consecutive rows and then skip 1 row. It is necessary to skip a row every so often because there are more rows per inch than stitches per inch. If you were to pick up a stitch in every row, when you started to knit these picked-up stitches, you would have too many stitches and the button bands would look wavy.

1. Place the work with the right side facing you. Starting at the right edge of your piece with the knitting needle in your right hand, place the needle in the first stitch, poking through from the outside to the inside. (Illus. A & B; F & G)

2. Loop the yarn under and around the needle and pull the needle back through that same stitch. There should be 1 stitch on the needle. (Illus. C & D; H & I)

3. Continue to poke the needle through each stitch, wrapping the yarn around the needle as if you were knitting and adding a stitch to the needle each time. (Illus. E & J)

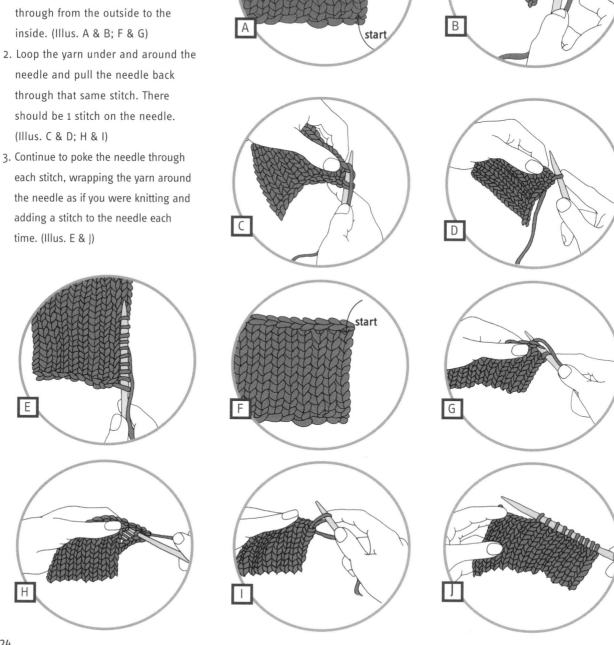

weaving in ends

Beginner knitters are often baffled by what to do with all the loose ends. Don't worry about them until you sew your projects together. While you are knitting, try to keep your ends about 4 inches long. Remember this when you are adding a new ball of yarn or casting on or binding off. If the ends are long enough, you can weave them in with a sewing needle. All you do is thread the needle with an end and weave the yarn back and forth through the seam 3 to 4 times. Then snip the end. You do not need to make a knot. If the ends are too short, you can use a crochet hook, but this is a bit harder.

blocking

Sometimes when a garment is completely assembled, it requires a bit of shaping. Blocking allows you to reshape the piece gently by applying steam, which relaxes the yarn fibers so they can be stretched in order to smooth out bulky seams, even out uneven knitting, or even enlarge a too-small garment.

Not every piece needs to be blocked; use your common sense. But if you do decide some reshaping or smoothing is in order, pin your garment onto a padded ironing board, easing it into the desired shape. If your iron can emit a strong stream of steam, hold the iron above the piece without touching it and saturate it with steam. Otherwise, dampen a towel, place it over the garment, and press with a warm iron. Allow the piece to remain pinned to the ironing board until it is completely cool.

Never apply a hot iron directly to a knitted piece, and always read the label on your yarn before blocking; some fibers should not be blocked.

SINGLE CROCHET AND SHRIMP STITCH

Even if you have never crocheted—and never plan to—it's useful to know a couple of basic crochet techniques for finishing off a knitted piece. Using a crochet stitch for edgings gives sweaters and throws a nice, polished look. Shrimp stitch gives a sturdy corded look. Generally, you want to use a crochet hook that matches the size knitting needle you used. For instance, if you used a size 6 knitting needle, you should use a size 6 (also known as size G) crochet hook.

single crochet

1. With the right side of the work facing you, insert your crochet hook through a stitch under the bind-off. (Illus. A)

2. Grab the yarn with the crochet hook and pull it through the stitch to the front of your work. (Illus. B) You will now have 1 loop on the crochet hook. (Illus. C)

3. Insert the crochet hook through the next stitch, hook the yarn, and pull it through the stitch. You now have 2 loops on the crochet hook. (Illus. D & E)

4. Hook the yarn and pull it through both of the loops on the crochet hook. (Illus. F) You will end up with 1 loop on the hook. Insert the hook through the next stitch and repeat across the entire row, ending with 1 loop on the hook.

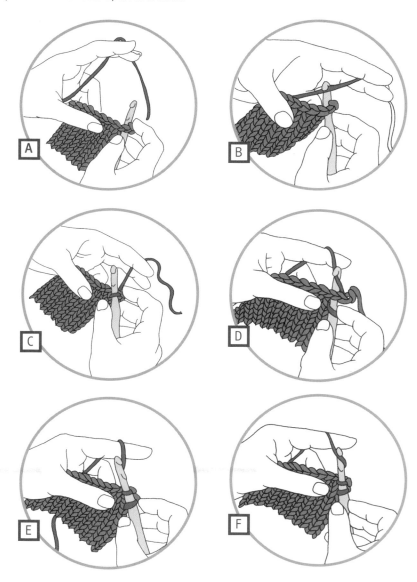

shrimp stitch

This is also known as backwards crochet because you work from left to right instead of right to left. You must do 1 row of single crochet (abbreviated **SC**) before you begin the shrimp stitch.

1. Make a slip stitch by grabbing the yarn through the loop on the hook. (Illus. A)

2. Keeping your right index finger on the loop, insert the hook into the next stitch to the right from the right side to the wrong side of the work. (Illus. B & C)

3. Grab the yarn with the hook and pull it through to the right side of the work. (Illus. D)

4. You should have 2 loops on the hook. (Illus. E)

5. Grab the yarn with the hook and pull it through the 2 loops. (Illus. F & G)

6. Repeat in the next stitch to the right. (Illus. H)

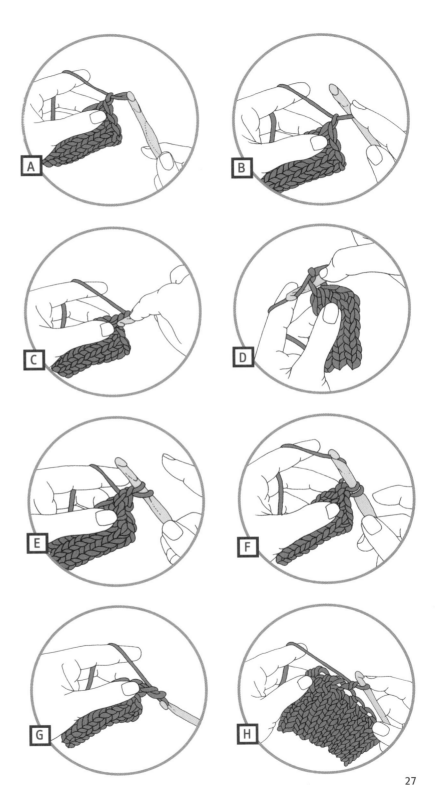

27

Project:

DATE BEGAN: _____

DATE COMPLETED: _____

PATTERN SOURCE: _____

WHO I MADE IT FOR: _____

NEEDLE SIZE: _____

SIZE AND MEASUREMENTS: _____

ADJUSTMENTS MADE: _____

COMMENTS: _____

_____

STITCHES PER INCH: _____ ROWS PER INCH: _____

ATTACH GAUGE SWATCH HERE

YARN LABEL AND YARN SAMPLE

PLACE PHOTO HERE

Project:

DATE BEGAN: _____

DATE COMPLETED: _____

PATTERN SOURCE: _____

WHO I MADE IT FOR: _____

NEEDLE SIZE: _____

SIZE AND MEASUREMENTS: _____

ADJUSTMENTS MADE: _____

COMMENTS: _____

_____

STITCHES PER INCH: _____ ROWS PER INCH: _____

ATTACH GAUGE SWATCH HERE

YARN LABEL AND YARN SAMPLE

PLACE PHOTO HERE

project:

DATE BEGAN: ⎯⎯⎯⎯⎯⎯⎯⎯⎯⎯⎯⎯⎯⎯⎯⎯

DATE COMPLETED: ⎯⎯⎯⎯⎯⎯⎯⎯⎯⎯⎯⎯⎯

PATTERN SOURCE: ⎯⎯⎯⎯⎯⎯⎯⎯⎯⎯⎯⎯⎯

WHO I MADE IT FOR: ⎯⎯⎯⎯⎯⎯⎯⎯⎯⎯⎯

NEEDLE SIZE: ⎯⎯⎯⎯⎯⎯⎯⎯⎯⎯⎯⎯⎯⎯⎯

SIZE AND MEASUREMENTS: ⎯⎯⎯⎯⎯⎯⎯⎯

ADJUSTMENTS MADE: ⎯⎯⎯⎯⎯⎯⎯⎯⎯⎯⎯

COMMENTS: ⎯⎯⎯⎯⎯⎯⎯⎯⎯⎯⎯⎯⎯⎯⎯

⎯⎯⎯⎯⎯⎯⎯⎯⎯⎯⎯⎯⎯⎯⎯⎯⎯⎯⎯⎯⎯⎯⎯⎯

STITCHES PER INCH: ⎯⎯⎯⎯⎯ ROWS PER INCH: ⎯⎯⎯⎯⎯⎯

ATTACH GAUGE SWATCH HERE

YARN LABEL AND YARN SAMPLE

PLACE PHOTO HERE

Project:

DATE BEGAN: _____

DATE COMPLETED: _____

PATTERN SOURCE: _____

WHO I MADE IT FOR: _____

NEEDLE SIZE: _____

SIZE AND MEASUREMENTS: _____

ADJUSTMENTS MADE: _____

COMMENTS: _____

_____

STITCHES PER INCH: _____ ROWS PER INCH: _____

ATTACH GAUGE SWATCH HERE

YARN LABEL AND YARN SAMPLE

PLACE PHOTO HERE

project:

DATE BEGAN: _____

DATE COMPLETED: _____

PATTERN SOURCE: _____

WHO I MADE IT FOR: _____

NEEDLE SIZE: _____

SIZE AND MEASUREMENTS: _____

ADJUSTMENTS MADE: _____

COMMENTS: _____

_____

STITCHES PER INCH: _____ ROWS PER INCH: _____

ATTACH GAUGE SWATCH HERE

YARN LABEL AND YARN SAMPLE

PLACE PHOTO HERE

Project:

DATE BEGAN: _____

DATE COMPLETED: _____

PATTERN SOURCE: _____

WHO I MADE IT FOR: _____

NEEDLE SIZE: _____

SIZE AND MEASUREMENTS: _____

ADJUSTMENTS MADE: _____

COMMENTS: _____

_____

STITCHES PER INCH:_____ ROWS PER INCH:_____

ATTACH GAUGE SWATCH HERE

YARN LABEL AND YARN SAMPLE

PLACE PHOTO HERE

Project:

DATE BEGAN: _____

DATE COMPLETED: _____

PATTERN SOURCE: _____

WHO I MADE IT FOR: _____

NEEDLE SIZE: _____

SIZE AND MEASUREMENTS: _____

ADJUSTMENTS MADE: _____

COMMENTS: _____

_____

STITCHES PER INCH: _____ ROWS PER INCH: _____

ATTACH GAUGE SWATCH HERE

YARN LABEL AND YARN SAMPLE

PLACE PHOTO HERE

project:

DATE BEGAN: _____

DATE COMPLETED: _____

PATTERN SOURCE: _____

WHO I MADE IT FOR: _____

NEEDLE SIZE: _____

SIZE AND MEASUREMENTS: _____

ADJUSTMENTS MADE: _____

COMMENTS: _____

_____

STITCHES PER INCH: _____ ROWS PER INCH: _____

ATTACH GAUGE SWATCH HERE

YARN LABEL AND YARN SAMPLE

PLACE PHOTO HERE

Project:

DATE BEGAN: ————————————

DATE COMPLETED: ————————————

PATTERN SOURCE: ————————————

WHO I MADE IT FOR: ————————————

NEEDLE SIZE: ————————————

SIZE AND MEASUREMENTS: ————————————

ADJUSTMENTS MADE: ————————————

COMMENTS: ————————————

————————————

STITCHES PER INCH: ———————ROWS PER INCH: ———————

ATTACH GAUGE SWATCH HERE

YARN LABEL AND YARN SAMPLE

PLACE PHOTO HERE

Project:

DATE BEGAN: _____

DATE COMPLETED: _____

PATTERN SOURCE: _____

WHO I MADE IT FOR: _____

NEEDLE SIZE: _____

SIZE AND MEASUREMENTS: _____

ADJUSTMENTS MADE: _____

COMMENTS: _____

_____

STITCHES PER INCH: _____ ROWS PER INCH: _____

ATTACH GAUGE SWATCH HERE

YARN LABEL AND YARN SAMPLE

PLACE PHOTO HERE

Project:

DATE BEGAN: _____

DATE COMPLETED: _____

PATTERN SOURCE: _____

WHO I MADE IT FOR: _____

NEEDLE SIZE: _____

SIZE AND MEASUREMENTS: _____

ADJUSTMENTS MADE: _____

COMMENTS: _____

_____

STITCHES PER INCH: _____ ROWS PER INCH: _____

ATTACH GAUGE SWATCH HERE

YARN LABEL AND YARN SAMPLE

PLACE PHOTO HERE

Project:

DATE BEGAN: ⎯⎯⎯⎯⎯⎯⎯⎯⎯⎯⎯⎯⎯⎯⎯⎯⎯

DATE COMPLETED: ⎯⎯⎯⎯⎯⎯⎯⎯⎯⎯⎯⎯⎯

PATTERN SOURCE: ⎯⎯⎯⎯⎯⎯⎯⎯⎯⎯⎯⎯⎯

WHO I MADE IT FOR: ⎯⎯⎯⎯⎯⎯⎯⎯⎯⎯⎯

NEEDLE SIZE: ⎯⎯⎯⎯⎯⎯⎯⎯⎯⎯⎯⎯⎯⎯⎯

SIZE AND MEASUREMENTS: ⎯⎯⎯⎯⎯⎯⎯⎯

ADJUSTMENTS MADE: ⎯⎯⎯⎯⎯⎯⎯⎯⎯⎯

COMMENTS: ⎯⎯⎯⎯⎯⎯⎯⎯⎯⎯⎯⎯⎯⎯

⎯⎯⎯⎯⎯⎯⎯⎯⎯⎯⎯⎯⎯⎯⎯⎯⎯⎯⎯⎯⎯⎯⎯⎯

STITCHES PER INCH: ⎯⎯⎯⎯⎯ ROWS PER INCH: ⎯⎯⎯⎯⎯⎯

ATTACH GAUGE SWATCH HERE

YARN LABEL AND YARN SAMPLE

PLACE PHOTO HERE

Project:

DATE BEGAN: _____

DATE COMPLETED: _____

PATTERN SOURCE: _____

WHO I MADE IT FOR: _____

NEEDLE SIZE: _____

SIZE AND MEASUREMENTS: _____

ADJUSTMENTS MADE: _____

COMMENTS: _____

_____

STITCHES PER INCH: _____ ROWS PER INCH: _____

ATTACH GAUGE SWATCH HERE

YARN LABEL AND YARN SAMPLE

PLACE PHOTO HERE

project:

DATE BEGAN: _____

DATE COMPLETED: _____

PATTERN SOURCE: _____

WHO I MADE IT FOR: _____

NEEDLE SIZE: _____

SIZE AND MEASUREMENTS: _____

ADJUSTMENTS MADE: _____

COMMENTS: _____

_____

STITCHES PER INCH: _____ ROWS PER INCH: _____

ATTACH GAUGE SWATCH HERE

YARN LABEL AND YARN SAMPLE

PLACE PHOTO HERE

Project:

DATE BEGAN: ——————————————

DATE COMPLETED: ——————————————

PATTERN SOURCE: ——————————————

WHO I MADE IT FOR: ——————————————

NEEDLE SIZE: ——————————————

SIZE AND MEASUREMENTS: ——————————————

ADJUSTMENTS MADE: ——————————————

COMMENTS: ——————————————

——————————————

STITCHES PER INCH:————— ROWS PER INCH:—————

ATTACH GAUGE SWATCH HERE

YARN LABEL AND YARN SAMPLE

PLACE PHOTO HERE

Project:

DATE BEGAN: —————————————————

DATE COMPLETED: —————————————

PATTERN SOURCE: —————————————

WHO I MADE IT FOR: ————————————

NEEDLE SIZE: —————————————————

SIZE AND MEASUREMENTS: ————————

ADJUSTMENTS MADE: ——————————————

COMMENTS: ————————————————————

STITCHES PER INCH: ————— ROWS PER INCH: ——————————

ATTACH GAUGE SWATCH HERE

YARN LABEL AND YARN SAMPLE

PLACE PHOTO HERE

Project:

DATE BEGAN: _____

DATE COMPLETED: _____

PATTERN SOURCE: _____

WHO I MADE IT FOR: _____

NEEDLE SIZE: _____

SIZE AND MEASUREMENTS: _____

ADJUSTMENTS MADE: _____

COMMENTS: _____

_____

STITCHES PER INCH: _____ ROWS PER INCH: _____

ATTACH GAUGE SWATCH HERE

YARN LABEL AND YARN SAMPLE

PLACE PHOTO HERE

Project:

DATE BEGAN: _____

DATE COMPLETED: _____

PATTERN SOURCE: _____

WHO I MADE IT FOR: _____

NEEDLE SIZE: _____

SIZE AND MEASUREMENTS: _____

ADJUSTMENTS MADE: _____

COMMENTS: _____

_____

STITCHES PER INCH: _____ ROWS PER INCH: _____

ATTACH GAUGE SWATCH HERE

YARN LABEL AND YARN SAMPLE

PLACE PHOTO HERE

Project:

DATE BEGAN: _____

DATE COMPLETED: _____

PATTERN SOURCE: _____

WHO I MADE IT FOR: _____

NEEDLE SIZE: _____

SIZE AND MEASUREMENTS: _____

ADJUSTMENTS MADE: _____

COMMENTS: _____

_____

STITCHES PER INCH: _____ ROWS PER INCH: _____

ATTACH GAUGE SWATCH HERE

YARN LABEL AND YARN SAMPLE

PLACE PHOTO HERE

Project:

DATE BEGAN: ———————————————

DATE COMPLETED: ———————————————

PATTERN SOURCE: ———————————————

WHO I MADE IT FOR: ———————————————

NEEDLE SIZE: ———————————————

SIZE AND MEASUREMENTS: ———————————————

ADJUSTMENTS MADE: ———————————————

COMMENTS: ———————————————

———————————————

STITCHES PER INCH: —————— ROWS PER INCH: ——————

ATTACH GAUGE SWATCH HERE

YARN LABEL AND YARN SAMPLE

PLACE PHOTO HERE

Project:

DATE BEGAN: _____

DATE COMPLETED: _____

PATTERN SOURCE: _____

WHO I MADE IT FOR: _____

NEEDLE SIZE: _____

SIZE AND MEASUREMENTS: _____

ADJUSTMENTS MADE: _____

COMMENTS: _____

_____

STITCHES PER INCH: _____ ROWS PER INCH: _____

ATTACH GAUGE SWATCH HERE

YARN LABEL AND YARN SAMPLE

PLACE PHOTO HERE

project:

DATE BEGAN: _____

DATE COMPLETED: _____

PATTERN SOURCE: _____

WHO I MADE IT FOR: _____

NEEDLE SIZE: _____

SIZE AND MEASUREMENTS: _____

ADJUSTMENTS MADE: _____

COMMENTS: _____

_____

STITCHES PER INCH:_____ ROWS PER INCH:_____

ATTACH GAUGE SWATCH HERE

YARN LABEL AND YARN SAMPLE

PLACE PHOTO HERE

project:

DATE BEGAN: _____

DATE COMPLETED: _____

PATTERN SOURCE: _____

WHO I MADE IT FOR: _____

NEEDLE SIZE: _____

SIZE AND MEASUREMENTS: _____

ADJUSTMENTS MADE: _____

COMMENTS: _____

_____

STITCHES PER INCH: _____ ROWS PER INCH: _____

ATTACH GAUGE SWATCH HERE

YARN LABEL AND YARN SAMPLE

PLACE PHOTO HERE

Project:

DATE BEGAN: _____

DATE COMPLETED: _____

PATTERN SOURCE: _____

WHO I MADE IT FOR: _____

NEEDLE SIZE: _____

SIZE AND MEASUREMENTS: _____

ADJUSTMENTS MADE: _____

COMMENTS: _____

_____

STITCHES PER INCH:_____ ROWS PER INCH:_____

ATTACH GAUGE SWATCH HERE

YARN LABEL AND YARN SAMPLE

PLACE PHOTO HERE

Project:

DATE BEGAN: _____

DATE COMPLETED: _____

PATTERN SOURCE: _____

WHO I MADE IT FOR: _____

NEEDLE SIZE: _____

SIZE AND MEASUREMENTS: _____

ADJUSTMENTS MADE: _____

COMMENTS: _____

_____

STITCHES PER INCH: _____ ROWS PER INCH: _____

ATTACH GAUGE SWATCH HERE

YARN LABEL AND YARN SAMPLE

PLACE PHOTO HERE

Project:

DATE BEGAN: _____

DATE COMPLETED: _____

PATTERN SOURCE: _____

WHO I MADE IT FOR: _____

NEEDLE SIZE: _____

SIZE AND MEASUREMENTS: _____

ADJUSTMENTS MADE: _____

COMMENTS: _____

_____

STITCHES PER INCH: _____ ROWS PER INCH: _____

ATTACH GAUGE SWATCH HERE

YARN LABEL AND YARN SAMPLE

PLACE PHOTO HERE

Project:

DATE BEGAN: _____

DATE COMPLETED: _____

PATTERN SOURCE: _____

WHO I MADE IT FOR: _____

NEEDLE SIZE: _____

SIZE AND MEASUREMENTS: _____

ADJUSTMENTS MADE: _____

COMMENTS: _____

_____

STITCHES PER INCH: _____ ROWS PER INCH: _____

ATTACH GAUGE SWATCH HERE

YARN LABEL AND YARN SAMPLE

PLACE PHOTO HERE

project:

DATE BEGAN: _____

DATE COMPLETED: _____

PATTERN SOURCE: _____

WHO I MADE IT FOR: _____

NEEDLE SIZE: _____

SIZE AND MEASUREMENTS: _____

ADJUSTMENTS MADE: _____

COMMENTS: _____

_____

STITCHES PER INCH: _____ ROWS PER INCH: _____

ATTACH GAUGE SWATCH HERE

YARN LABEL AND YARN SAMPLE

PLACE PHOTO HERE

project:

DATE BEGAN: _____

DATE COMPLETED: _____

PATTERN SOURCE: _____

WHO I MADE IT FOR: _____

NEEDLE SIZE: _____

SIZE AND MEASUREMENTS: _____

ADJUSTMENTS MADE: _____

COMMENTS: _____

_____

STITCHES PER INCH: _____ ROWS PER INCH: _____

ATTACH GAUGE SWATCH HERE

YARN LABEL AND YARN SAMPLE

PLACE PHOTO HERE

Project:

DATE BEGAN: _____

DATE COMPLETED: _____

PATTERN SOURCE: _____

WHO I MADE IT FOR: _____

NEEDLE SIZE: _____

SIZE AND MEASUREMENTS: _____

ADJUSTMENTS MADE: _____

COMMENTS: _____

_____

STITCHES PER INCH: _____ ROWS PER INCH: _____

ATTACH GAUGE SWATCH HERE

YARN LABEL AND YARN SAMPLE

PLACE PHOTO HERE

Project:

DATE BEGAN: ───────────────────

DATE COMPLETED: ───────────────────

PATTERN SOURCE: ───────────────────

WHO I MADE IT FOR: ───────────────────

NEEDLE SIZE: ───────────────────

SIZE AND MEASUREMENTS: ───────────────

ADJUSTMENTS MADE: ───────────────────

COMMENTS: ───────────────────

───────────────────

STITCHES PER INCH: _____ ROWS PER INCH: _____

ATTACH GAUGE SWATCH HERE

YARN LABEL AND YARN SAMPLE

PLACE PHOTO HERE

project:

DATE BEGAN: _____

DATE COMPLETED: _____

PATTERN SOURCE: _____

WHO I MADE IT FOR: _____

NEEDLE SIZE: _____

SIZE AND MEASUREMENTS: _____

ADJUSTMENTS MADE: _____

COMMENTS: _____

_____

STITCHES PER INCH: _____ ROWS PER INCH: _____

ATTACH GAUGE SWATCH HERE

YARN LABEL AND YARN SAMPLE

PLACE PHOTO HERE

Project:

DATE BEGAN: _____

DATE COMPLETED: _____

PATTERN SOURCE: _____

WHO I MADE IT FOR: _____

NEEDLE SIZE: _____

SIZE AND MEASUREMENTS: _____

ADJUSTMENTS MADE: _____

COMMENTS: _____

_____

STITCHES PER INCH: _____ ROWS PER INCH: _____

ATTACH GAUGE SWATCH HERE

YARN LABEL AND YARN SAMPLE

PLACE PHOTO HERE

Project:

DATE BEGAN: _____

DATE COMPLETED: _____

PATTERN SOURCE: _____

WHO I MADE IT FOR: _____

NEEDLE SIZE: _____

SIZE AND MEASUREMENTS: _____

ADJUSTMENTS MADE: _____

COMMENTS: _____

_____

STITCHES PER INCH:_____ROWS PER INCH:_____

ATTACH GAUGE SWATCH HERE

YARN LABEL AND YARN SAMPLE

PLACE PHOTO HERE

Project:

DATE BEGAN: _____

DATE COMPLETED: _____

PATTERN SOURCE: _____

WHO I MADE IT FOR: _____

NEEDLE SIZE: _____

SIZE AND MEASUREMENTS: _____

ADJUSTMENTS MADE: _____

COMMENTS: _____

_____

STITCHES PER INCH: _____ ROWS PER INCH: _____

ATTACH GAUGE SWATCH HERE

YARN LABEL AND YARN SAMPLE

PLACE PHOTO HERE

Project:

DATE BEGAN: ⎯⎯⎯⎯⎯⎯⎯⎯⎯⎯⎯⎯⎯

DATE COMPLETED: ⎯⎯⎯⎯⎯⎯⎯⎯⎯⎯⎯

PATTERN SOURCE: ⎯⎯⎯⎯⎯⎯⎯⎯⎯⎯⎯

WHO I MADE IT FOR: ⎯⎯⎯⎯⎯⎯⎯⎯⎯

NEEDLE SIZE: ⎯⎯⎯⎯⎯⎯⎯⎯⎯⎯⎯⎯

SIZE AND MEASUREMENTS: ⎯⎯⎯⎯⎯⎯⎯

ADJUSTMENTS MADE: ⎯⎯⎯⎯⎯⎯⎯⎯⎯

COMMENTS: ⎯⎯⎯⎯⎯⎯⎯⎯⎯⎯⎯⎯

⎯⎯⎯⎯⎯⎯⎯⎯⎯⎯⎯⎯⎯⎯⎯⎯⎯⎯⎯

STITCHES PER INCH:⎯⎯⎯⎯ROWS PER INCH:⎯⎯⎯⎯

ATTACH GAUGE SWATCH HERE

YARN LABEL AND YARN SAMPLE

PLACE PHOTO HERE

project:

DATE BEGAN: _____

DATE COMPLETED: _____

PATTERN SOURCE: _____

WHO I MADE IT FOR: _____

NEEDLE SIZE: _____

SIZE AND MEASUREMENTS: _____

ADJUSTMENTS MADE: _____

COMMENTS: _____

_____

STITCHES PER INCH:_____ ROWS PER INCH:_____

ATTACH GAUGE SWATCH HERE

YARN LABEL AND YARN SAMPLE

PLACE PHOTO HERE

Project:

DATE BEGAN: _____

DATE COMPLETED: _____

PATTERN SOURCE: _____

WHO I MADE IT FOR: _____

NEEDLE SIZE: _____

SIZE AND MEASUREMENTS: _____

ADJUSTMENTS MADE: _____

COMMENTS: _____

_____

STITCHES PER INCH: _____ ROWS PER INCH: _____

ATTACH GAUGE SWATCH HERE

YARN LABEL AND YARN SAMPLE

PLACE PHOTO HERE

Project:

DATE BEGAN: —————————————————

DATE COMPLETED: ————————————————

PATTERN SOURCE: ————————————————

WHO I MADE IT FOR: ———————————————

NEEDLE SIZE: —————————————————

SIZE AND MEASUREMENTS: —————————————

ADJUSTMENTS MADE: ——————————————

COMMENTS: ——————————————————

—————————————————————

STITCHES PER INCH: ————— ROWS PER INCH: —————

ATTACH GAUGE SWATCH HERE

YARN LABEL AND YARN SAMPLE

PLACE PHOTO HERE

Project:

DATE BEGAN: _____

DATE COMPLETED: _____

PATTERN SOURCE: _____

WHO I MADE IT FOR: _____

NEEDLE SIZE: _____

SIZE AND MEASUREMENTS: _____

ADJUSTMENTS MADE: _____

COMMENTS: _____

_____

STITCHES PER INCH: _____ ROWS PER INCH: _____

ATTACH GAUGE SWATCH HERE

YARN LABEL AND YARN SAMPLE

PLACE PHOTO HERE

project:

DATE BEGAN: _____

DATE COMPLETED: _____

PATTERN SOURCE: _____

WHO I MADE IT FOR: _____

NEEDLE SIZE: _____

SIZE AND MEASUREMENTS: _____

ADJUSTMENTS MADE: _____

COMMENTS: _____

_____

STITCHES PER INCH: _____ ROWS PER INCH: _____

ATTACH GAUGE SWATCH HERE

YARN LABEL AND YARN SAMPLE

PLACE PHOTO HERE

Project:

DATE BEGAN: _____

DATE COMPLETED: _____

PATTERN SOURCE: _____

WHO I MADE IT FOR: _____

NEEDLE SIZE: _____

SIZE AND MEASUREMENTS: _____

ADJUSTMENTS MADE: _____

COMMENTS: _____

_____

STITCHES PER INCH: _____ ROWS PER INCH: _____

ATTACH GAUGE SWATCH HERE

YARN LABEL AND YARN SAMPLE

PLACE PHOTO HERE

Project:

DATE BEGAN: _____

DATE COMPLETED: _____

PATTERN SOURCE: _____

WHO I MADE IT FOR: _____

NEEDLE SIZE: _____

SIZE AND MEASUREMENTS: _____

ADJUSTMENTS MADE: _____

COMMENTS: _____

_____

STITCHES PER INCH: _____ ROWS PER INCH: _____

ATTACH GAUGE SWATCH HERE

YARN LABEL AND YARN SAMPLE

PLACE PHOTO HERE

project:

DATE BEGAN: _____

DATE COMPLETED: _____

PATTERN SOURCE: _____

WHO I MADE IT FOR: _____

NEEDLE SIZE: _____

SIZE AND MEASUREMENTS: _____

ADJUSTMENTS MADE: _____

COMMENTS: _____

_____

STITCHES PER INCH: _____ ROWS PER INCH: _____

ATTACH GAUGE SWATCH HERE

YARN LABEL AND YARN SAMPLE

PLACE PHOTO HERE

Project:

DATE BEGAN: _____

DATE COMPLETED: _____

PATTERN SOURCE: _____

WHO I MADE IT FOR: _____

NEEDLE SIZE: _____

SIZE AND MEASUREMENTS: _____

ADJUSTMENTS MADE: _____

COMMENTS: _____

_____

STITCHES PER INCH: _____ ROWS PER INCH: _____

ATTACH GAUGE SWATCH HERE

YARN LABEL AND YARN SAMPLE

PLACE PHOTO HERE

Project:

DATE BEGAN: ——————————————

DATE COMPLETED: ——————————

PATTERN SOURCE: ——————————

WHO I MADE IT FOR: ————————

NEEDLE SIZE: ————————————

SIZE AND MEASUREMENTS: ————

ADJUSTMENTS MADE: ————————

COMMENTS: ——————————————

————————————————————

STITCHES PER INCH:————————ROWS PER INCH:————————

ATTACH GAUGE SWATCH HERE

YARN LABEL AND YARN SAMPLE

PLACE PHOTO HERE

Project:

DATE BEGAN: _____

DATE COMPLETED: _____

PATTERN SOURCE: _____

WHO I MADE IT FOR: _____

NEEDLE SIZE: _____

SIZE AND MEASUREMENTS: _____

ADJUSTMENTS MADE: _____

COMMENTS: _____

_____

STITCHES PER INCH: _____ ROWS PER INCH: _____

ATTACH GAUGE SWATCH HERE

YARN LABEL AND YARN SAMPLE

PLACE PHOTO HERE

Project:

DATE BEGAN: _____

DATE COMPLETED: _____

PATTERN SOURCE: _____

WHO I MADE IT FOR: _____

NEEDLE SIZE: _____

SIZE AND MEASUREMENTS: _____

ADJUSTMENTS MADE: _____

COMMENTS: _____

_____

STITCHES PER INCH: _____ ROWS PER INCH: _____

ATTACH GAUGE SWATCH HERE

YARN LABEL AND YARN SAMPLE

PLACE PHOTO HERE

project:

DATE BEGAN: _____

DATE COMPLETED: _____

PATTERN SOURCE: _____

WHO I MADE IT FOR: _____

NEEDLE SIZE: _____

SIZE AND MEASUREMENTS: _____

ADJUSTMENTS MADE: _____

COMMENTS: _____

_____

STITCHES PER INCH: _____ ROWS PER INCH: _____

ATTACH GAUGE SWATCH HERE

YARN LABEL AND YARN SAMPLE

PLACE PHOTO HERE

project:

DATE BEGAN: _____

DATE COMPLETED: _____

PATTERN SOURCE: _____

WHO I MADE IT FOR: _____

NEEDLE SIZE: _____

SIZE AND MEASUREMENTS: _____

ADJUSTMENTS MADE: _____

COMMENTS: _____

_____

STITCHES PER INCH: _____ ROWS PER INCH: _____

ATTACH GAUGE SWATCH HERE

YARN LABEL AND YARN SAMPLE

PLACE PHOTO HERE

Project:

DATE BEGAN: _____

DATE COMPLETED: _____

PATTERN SOURCE: _____

WHO I MADE IT FOR: _____

NEEDLE SIZE: _____

SIZE AND MEASUREMENTS: _____

ADJUSTMENTS MADE: _____

COMMENTS: _____

_____

STITCHES PER INCH: _____ ROWS PER INCH: _____

ATTACH GAUGE SWATCH HERE

YARN LABEL AND YARN SAMPLE

PLACE PHOTO HERE

Project:

DATE BEGAN: _____

DATE COMPLETED: _____

PATTERN SOURCE: _____

WHO I MADE IT FOR: _____

NEEDLE SIZE: _____

SIZE AND MEASUREMENTS: _____

ADJUSTMENTS MADE: _____

COMMENTS: _____

_____

STITCHES PER INCH: _____ ROWS PER INCH: _____

ATTACH GAUGE SWATCH HERE

YARN LABEL AND YARN SAMPLE

PLACE PHOTO HERE

Project:

DATE BEGAN: _____

DATE COMPLETED: _____

PATTERN SOURCE: _____

WHO I MADE IT FOR: _____

NEEDLE SIZE: _____

SIZE AND MEASUREMENTS: _____

ADJUSTMENTS MADE: _____

COMMENTS: _____

_____

STITCHES PER INCH: _____ ROWS PER INCH: _____

ATTACH GAUGE SWATCH HERE

YARN LABEL AND YARN SAMPLE

PLACE PHOTO HERE

project:

DATE BEGAN: ———————————————————

DATE COMPLETED: ——————————————————

PATTERN SOURCE: ——————————————————

WHO I MADE IT FOR: —————————————————

NEEDLE SIZE: ———————————————————

SIZE AND MEASUREMENTS: ————————————————

ADJUSTMENTS MADE: ——————————————————

COMMENTS: ————————————————————

———————————————————————

STITCHES PER INCH:————————ROWS PER INCH:——————————

ATTACH GAUGE SWATCH HERE

YARN LABEL AND YARN SAMPLE

PLACE PHOTO HERE

project:

DATE BEGAN: —————————————————

DATE COMPLETED: ———————————————

PATTERN SOURCE: ———————————————

WHO I MADE IT FOR: ——————————————

NEEDLE SIZE: ————————————————

SIZE AND MEASUREMENTS: —————————————

ADJUSTMENTS MADE: ———————————————

COMMENTS: —————————————————

STITCHES PER INCH: —————— ROWS PER INCH: ——————

ATTACH GAUGE SWATCH HERE

YARN LABEL AND YARN SAMPLE

PLACE PHOTO HERE

Project:

DATE BEGAN: _____

DATE COMPLETED: _____

PATTERN SOURCE: _____

WHO I MADE IT FOR: _____

NEEDLE SIZE: _____

SIZE AND MEASUREMENTS: _____

ADJUSTMENTS MADE: _____

COMMENTS: _____

_____

STITCHES PER INCH: _____ ROWS PER INCH: _____

ATTACH GAUGE SWATCH HERE

YARN LABEL AND YARN SAMPLE

PLACE PHOTO HERE

Project:

DATE BEGAN: _____

DATE COMPLETED: _____

PATTERN SOURCE: _____

WHO I MADE IT FOR: _____

NEEDLE SIZE: _____

SIZE AND MEASUREMENTS: _____

ADJUSTMENTS MADE: _____

COMMENTS: _____

_____

STITCHES PER INCH: _____ ROWS PER INCH: _____

ATTACH GAUGE SWATCH HERE

YARN LABEL AND YARN SAMPLE

PLACE PHOTO HERE

project:

DATE BEGAN: _____

DATE COMPLETED: _____

PATTERN SOURCE: _____

WHO I MADE IT FOR: _____

NEEDLE SIZE: _____

SIZE AND MEASUREMENTS: _____

ADJUSTMENTS MADE: _____

COMMENTS: _____

_____

STITCHES PER INCH: _____ ROWS PER INCH: _____

ATTACH GAUGE SWATCH HERE

YARN LABEL AND YARN SAMPLE

PLACE PHOTO HERE

project:

DATE BEGAN: _____

DATE COMPLETED: _____

PATTERN SOURCE: _____

WHO I MADE IT FOR: _____

NEEDLE SIZE: _____

SIZE AND MEASUREMENTS: _____

ADJUSTMENTS MADE: _____

COMMENTS: _____

_____

STITCHES PER INCH: _____ ROWS PER INCH: _____

ATTACH GAUGE SWATCH HERE

YARN LABEL AND YARN SAMPLE

PLACE PHOTO HERE

Project:

DATE BEGAN: _____

DATE COMPLETED: _____

PATTERN SOURCE: _____

WHO I MADE IT FOR: _____

NEEDLE SIZE: _____

SIZE AND MEASUREMENTS: _____

ADJUSTMENTS MADE: _____

COMMENTS: _____

_____

STITCHES PER INCH: _____ ROWS PER INCH: _____

ATTACH GAUGE SWATCH HERE

YARN LABEL AND YARN SAMPLE

PLACE PHOTO HERE

Project:

DATE BEGAN: _____

DATE COMPLETED: _____

PATTERN SOURCE: _____

WHO I MADE IT FOR: _____

NEEDLE SIZE: _____

SIZE AND MEASUREMENTS: _____

ADJUSTMENTS MADE: _____

COMMENTS: _____

_____

STITCHES PER INCH: _____ ROWS PER INCH: _____

ATTACH GAUGE SWATCH HERE

YARN LABEL AND YARN SAMPLE

PLACE PHOTO HERE

Project:

DATE BEGAN: _____

DATE COMPLETED: _____

PATTERN SOURCE: _____

WHO I MADE IT FOR: _____

NEEDLE SIZE: _____

SIZE AND MEASUREMENTS: _____

ADJUSTMENTS MADE: _____

COMMENTS: _____

_____

STITCHES PER INCH: _____ ROWS PER INCH: _____

ATTACH GAUGE SWATCH HERE

YARN LABEL AND YARN SAMPLE

PLACE PHOTO HERE

GAUGE PAGE

THE MOST IMPORTANT MESSAGE HERE IS THAT **YOU MUST ALWAYS MAKE A GAUGE SWATCH!** IF YOU DON'T MAKE A GAUGE SWATCH, THERE ARE NO GUARANTEES THAT YOUR SWEATER WILL FIT PROPERLY!

STITCH GAUGE = THE NUMBER OF STITCHES REQUIRED TO PRODUCE 1 INCH OF KNITTED FABRIC

Here's how to check your gauge:

- Cast on 4 times the number of stitches required per inch. For example, if the gauge is 4 stitches = 1 inch, cast on 16 stitches; if your gauge is supposed to be 3 stitches = 1 inch, cast on 12 stitches.

- Work in the pattern stitch using the needle size recommended for the body of the sweater. Sometimes ribbing is knit on smaller needles, but you shouldn't use the smaller size for your gauge.

- When your swatch is approximately 4 inches long, slip it off the needle and place it on a flat surface. Measure the width of your swatch. If it measures 4 inches wide, you're getting the required gauge and can begin your knitting project.

- If your swatch is more than 4 inches wide, your knitting is too loose. Reknit your swatch on needles a size or two smaller and measure again. Repeat as necessary, using smaller needles until you get the correct gauge.

- If your swatch is less than 4 inches wide, you are knitting too tight. Reknit your swatch on needles a size or two larger and measure the swatch again. Repeat as necessary, using larger needles until you get the correct gauge.

You should also know that gauge can change as you make your garment. This happens for a multitude of reasons and does not mean you are a bad knitter. Please check the width of what you are knitting once the piece measures about 3 inches long. Compare it to the measurements the pattern provides and make adjustments in the needle size if necessary.

REMEMBER

Always knit a gauge swatch–*Always!!*

HELPFUL HINTS

Keep these hints in mind as you knit—you might save yourself from ripping out rows of stitches or untangling a gaggle of knots.

USING MULTIPLE STRANDS OF YARN

Some patterns call for more than one strand of yarn. This means you knit with two or more strands of yarn as though they were one. You would do this because you really liked a certain yarn, but it wasn't thick enough as a single strand. To use multiple strands of yarn, you can wind the separate balls into one ball. We find this easier than working from two or more balls at once. You do not need to hold the yarn any differently. Work as though there is one strand. Do not worry if the strands twist.

ATTACHING NEW YARN WHEN SHAPING THE NECK FOR A PULLOVER

When you have finished binding off for one side of a neck on a V-neck or crew-neck pullover, you will be instructed to attach the yarn and continue binding off on the other side of the neck. Make sure you attach the yarn in the center of the sweater and not at the outside or shoulder edge.

INCREASING ON SLEEVES

You can begin to increase on sleeves on the row after the ribbing. If there is a rolled edge, you can begin after 4 rows. When the instructions tell you to increase every 4th row, this means after the first time you increase. You do not need to work 4 rows after the ribbing and then begin to increase.

This is where your increasing should occur on a stockinette sweater where you are increasing every 4th row:

Row 1: Knit–Increase

Row 2: Purl

Row 3: Knit

Row 4: Purl

Repeat rows 1–4 until the required number of increases have been worked.

THE FOLLOWING ARE TERMS YOU MAY ENCOUNTER IN KNITTING PATTERNS

KNITTING MARKERS

When you need to mark off a designated number of stitches on your needle—say, to mark the center of a V-neck—you may be instructed to place a marker on the needle. You can buy markers at your yarn shop or just make your own by tying a short strand of yarn in a color that contrasts with your piece into a loop.

REVERSE SHAPING

We use this term when we want you to make two pieces, one the mirror image of the other. When you shape the neck on a pullover, you bind off the center stitches and then finish one side of the sweater at a time. On one side you will have to shape the neckline in one direction (while knitting) and on the other side you will have to shape it in the other direction (while purling). Also, when you make a cardigan, you make two front sections—one that will be the right side when worn and one that will be the left side when worn—and must shape the necklines and armholes in opposite directions. The easiest way to visualize this is to shape one side without really thinking about it and then, when you get to the neck shaping on the second side, lay both pieces out as they would be on the finished sweater. You will see what the second neckline needs to look like.

YARDAGE

Yardage helps you determine how many balls of yarn you will need for your project. Many books and patterns tell you that you need a certain number of grams or ounces, but in our experience this is an inaccurate way to determine the amount of yarn you will need, as different fibers have different weights. Acrylic is a much lighter fiber than wool: A 50-gram ball of acrylic yarn might contain 200 yards, whereas a 50-gram ball of wool might contain only 125 yards. Therefore, if a pattern called for 200 grams of acrylic yarn and you bought 200 grams of wool instead, you would be 300 yards short.

KNITTING GLOSSARY

BIND OFF (CAST OFF) This is the way you get stitches off the needle at the end of a project. Cast off is also a method used to decrease stitches.

CAST ON This is how you put stitches onto your needle to begin a project

DEC. Decrease. This is how you take stitches away once you have begun knitting. We use two methods of decreasing in this book, SSK and K2tog.

EDGE STITCH An edge stitch is exactly what it sounds like: the stitch at the edge of your work. Some of our patterns call for an edge stitch, and this means that we want you to knit the first and last stitch on every row, no matter what the rest of the pattern requires.

GARTER STITCH Knit every row. But if you are knitting in the round (on a circular needle), then garter stitch means you should knit 1 round and purl the next.

INC. Increase. This is how you add a stitch onto your needle once you have begun knitting. We use two methods of increasing in this book, a bar increase (Make 1, abbreviated **M1**) and knitting into the front and back of a stitch.

K Knit.

K2TOG Knit 2 stitches together. This is a method of decreasing. It slants your decrease toward the right.

P Purl.

REV ST ST Reverse Stockinette Stitch. P1 row, K1 row, and the purl side is the right side of the garment.

RS Right side. This is the side that will face out when you are wearing the garment. In this book, the RS is always the knit side.

SC Single crochet.

SEED STITCH Seed stitch is like a messed-up ribbing. As for ribbing, you alternate knitting and purling, but instead of knitting on the knit stitches and purling on the purl stitches to create ribs, you purl over your knit stitches and knit over your purl stitches to create little "seeds."

SSK Slip, Slip, Knit. This is a method of decreasing. It slants your decrease toward the left.

ST ST Stockinette Stitch. K1 row, P1 row. But if you are knitting in the round (on a circular needle), then St st means you should knit every round.

WS Wrong Side. This is the side that will face in when you are wearing the garment. In St st, the WS is always the purl side.

YARN DOUBLED When you knit with the yarn doubled, you are working with 2 strands of yarn held together as though they were 1. Yarn tripled means working with 3 strands of yarn held together. It is no harder to knit with 2 or 3 strands of yarn than it is to knit with 1. When we tell you to use a yarn doubled or tripled, it means the yarn we used for the pattern needed to be thicker than it actually is in order to achieve the proper gauge. If you prefer not to double or triple yarn, try substituting a bulkier yarn that knits to the gauge with a single strand. Just remember that if you use a single strand of yarn where we used 2, you will need only half the yardage to complete the pattern, or one third if the yarn is tripled.

YO Yarn Over. This is how you make a hole in your work (on purpose).

..... n knitting patterns, asterisks are used to indicate that a series of stitches is to be repeated. Repeat only what is between the asterisks, not what is outside of them. For example, **K2, *(K2, P2)*** 3 times means K2, K2, P2, K2, P2, K2, P2. ***(K5, K2tog)* across row** means that you should K5, K2tog, K5, K2tog, and so on across the whole row.

NEEDLES

US	EURO MM	UK MM	NEW UK
0	2	14	2
1	2.5	13	2.25-2.5
2	2.5-3	12-11	2.75-3
3	3.5	10	3.25
4	3.5	-	3.5
5	3.5	9	3.75
6	4	8	4
7	4.5	7	4.5
8	5	6	5
9	5.5	5	5.5
10	6	4	6
10.5	6.5	3	6.5
11	8	0	8
13	9	00	9
15	10	000	10
17	2.5	-	-
19	15.5	-	-

YARN WEIGHTS

HEAVY WORSTED 4 stitches to the inch

CHUNKY 3 to 3½ stitches to the inch

SUPER CHUNKY 2 to 2½ stitches to the inch

EXTRA SUPER CHUNKY 1 to 1½ stitches to the inch

1
2
3
4
5
6
7
8

ALSO AVAILABLE

The Yarn Girls' Guide to Simple Knits
by Julie Carles and Jordana Jacobs
0-609-60880-0 $30.00 hardcover
(Canada: $45.00)

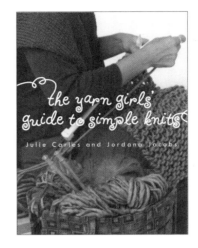

The Yarn Girls' Guide to Kid Knits
by Julie Carles and Jordana Jacobs
1-4000-5171-1 $30.00 hardcover
(Canada: $45.00)

Yarn Girls' Kid Knits Pattern Note Cards
1-4000-5397-8
$13.00 (Canada: $18.00)